Retirement Parachute

Unlock the Secrets to Secure Your Retirement and Guarantee Income for Life

Flavio Medeiros

6th Avenue Publishing

Copyright © 2023 Flavio Medeiros

All rights reserved.

No portion of this book may be reproduced in any form without written permission from the publisher or author, except as permitted by U.S. copyright law.

This book is in no way financial advice. Everyone's situation is different, so the best way to know what is right for you is to sit with a professional or do your own research.

Contents

1. Forward — 1
2. The Importance of Retirement Income Planning in Your 60's — 7
3. Social Security — 16
4. 2 Phases of Retirement — 23
5. Mitigating Market Risk In Your Retirement — 29
6. The Limitations of the 4% Rule for Retirement Income — 35
7. The Benefits of Rolling Over Old 401(k)s to IRAs — 42
8. What Is The Retirement Parachute? — 48

9. Retirement Healthcare: Preparing for and Managing Healthcare Costs in Retirement — 61

10. How to Protect and Transfer Your Wealth With Estate Planning — 68

11. Summary — 77

Afterword — 80

Forward

Welcome to "Retirement Parachute," your ultimate guide to securing your financial future and ensuring a lifetime of income in retirement. As you approach retirement age, it's natural to feel a sense of uncertainty about your financial future. That's where the "Retirement Parachute" comes in - it's a strategy that offers a guaranteed income stream throughout your golden years, no market risk, and still gives you growth potential of your money tied to market growth.

In this book, I'll show you how to leverage the power of the "Retirement Parachute" to protect your retirement savings and ensure a worry-free retirement. We'll explore the benefits of this unique financial product, including how it offers a balance of growth potential and protection against market volatility, and how to maximize your returns while minimizing risk.

Whether you're a seasoned investor or just starting to plan for retirement, "Retirement Parachute" is your essential guide to securing your financial future.

So if you're ready to take the leap and secure your financial future with the "Retirement Parachute," let's get started!

About Flavio

As a Financial Advisor with over 16 years of experience, Flavio Medeiros has seen firsthand the challenges that retirees face when it comes to securing a comfortable retirement.

That's why he has dedicated his career to helping people retire smart with a secure retirement. With a strong background in the insurance industry and a deep commitment to his clients, Flavio has become a trusted advisor to many retirees in the Myrtle Beach area, as well as Rhode Island, where he's originally from.

In Retirement Parachute, Flavio shares his expertise on helping retirees who want to balance risk and reward in their retirement portfolios. to have guaranteed income or perhaps leave a legacy to their family. Drawing on his experience as an industry professional and his passion for helping people, Flavio provides clear and practical guidance on how the Retirement Parachute can work for you.

With Flavio's insights and expertise, you'll gain the knowledge and confidence you need to make informed decisions about your retirement savings.

Flavio resides in Myrtle Beach with his wife, Dawn and 3 boys, Devin, Nathan, and Henry. He's a Navy Veteran who enjoys traveling, sports, and the beach.

Thank you for choosing Retirement Parachute as your guide to a secure and happy retirement.

With Thanks

I would like to take a moment to express my deep appreciation to three groups of people who have been instrumental in my career and in the creation of "Retirement Parachute."

First and foremost, I want to thank my wife Dawn for her unwavering support and understanding throughout my career in the insurance industry. The demands of this business can be very challenging, and her love and encouragement have been a source of strength and inspiration to me every step of the way. My 3 boys are also very supportive, and I love them for that and so much more!

I also want to thank Mark Medeiros, my business partner and great friend, for giving me the opportunity to once again realize my dreams in this business. Mark's vision and leadership have been critical to the success of our agency, and I am grateful for his support and partnership.

Finally, I want to express my sincere gratitude to all of my clients, past and present. It has been an honor and a privilege to serve you and to help you achieve your retirement goals. Your trust and confidence in me have been the driving force behind my work, and I am deeply grateful for the opportunity to be of service.

Thank you all for your support and encouragement. Without you, "Retirement Parachute" would not have been possible.

The Importance of Retirement Income Planning in Your 60's

As you approach your 60's, retirement may start to feel more like a reality than a far-off dream. It's a time of life when you have the opportunity to focus on the things that matter most to you, whether that's traveling, spending time with family, or pursuing a favorite hobby. But to make the most of your retirement years, it's important to start planning early and make sure you have a steady stream of income to support your lifestyle.

In this book, we'll explore different strategies for generating retirement income, with a focus on debunking some common myths when using the stock market for retirement income and security. We will discuss the concept of using the Retirement Parachute to provide a secure and reliable source of income. We'll also discuss other important retirement topics; including healthcare, taxes, and estate planning, to help you plan for a secure and enjoyable retirement.

Why Retirement Income Planning is So Important

Retirement income planning is crucial for several reasons. First, you need to make sure you have enough money to cover your basic living expenses in retirement. This includes things like housing, food, and healthcare, as well as any other regular expenses you may have.

Second, you want to make sure you have enough money to enjoy your retirement years and do the things you've always wanted to do. This may include travel, hobbies, or spending time with loved ones. Without a steady stream of income, you may be forced to cut back on the things that matter most to you.

Finally, retirement income planning is important because it can help you avoid running out of money in retirement. Many people are living longer than ever before, which means you may need to plan for a retirement that lasts 20 or 30 years, or more. By generating a reliable source of income, you can help ensure that you have enough money to last throughout your retirement years.

The Risks of Not Planning for Retirement Income

Fortunately many people in their 60's have saved enough for retirement, but lack a plan in place to generate retirement income. This can lead to several risks, including:

- Running out of money in retirement: Without a plan to generate retirement income, you may be forced to rely on Social Security or other sources of income that may not be enough to cover your expenses.

- Being forced to work longer: If you haven't saved enough for retirement, you may be forced to work longer than you had planned in order to make ends meet.

- Having to rely on others for financial support: If you don't have enough income in retirement, you may need to rely on family members or other sources of support to make ends meet.

These risks can be especially daunting for individuals who are already in their 60's and may not have as much time to make up for lost ground. However, it's never too late to start planning for retirement income, and there are many strategies you can use to help secure your financial future.

The Retirement Parachute: A Guide to Secure Your Retirement

One strategy for generating retirement income that we'll be discussing in this book is the Retirement Parachute. This concept refers to retirement income planning that involves using a mix of different financial instruments to generate a reliable stream of income.

The idea behind the retirement parachute is that you want to have sources that are guaranteed in order to produce your retirement income, just as you wouldn't want to jump off a plane with anything that wasn't guaranteed to land you safely. This may include Social Security, pensions, and annuities, as well as other investments.

Annuities are an especially important part of the retirement parachute, as they can provide a reliable source of income that is guaranteed for life. Annuities come in many different forms, including fixed annuities, variable annuities, and indexed annuities. Each type of annuity has its own unique features and benefits, and we'll be discussing these in more detail throughout the book.

In addition to the Retirement Parachute, we'll also be discussing other important retirement topics, such as:

- **Healthcare:** As you age, your healthcare needs may increase, and it's important to plan for these expenses. We'll be discussing strategies for managing healthcare costs in retirement, including Medicare and long-term care insurance.

- **Risk:** Risk is a significant concern to your portfolio in retirement. Just remember that 4% withdrawal rate out of $500k in savings is $20,000 of income each year, but that same bucket down to $400k, at the same 4%, will now only produce $16,000 of income each year.

- **Estate Planning**: Estate planning is important for ensuring that your assets are distributed according to your wishes after you pass away. We'll be discussing different estate planning strategies, including wills, trusts, and powers of attorney.

Throughout the book, we'll also be providing real-world examples and case studies to help illustrate the concepts we're discussing. We'll be exploring different scenarios and showing how the retirement parachute approach can be tailored to meet the unique needs and goals of each individual.

By the end of this book, our goal is for you to have a solid understanding of retirement income planning, and to feel confident in your ability to create a retirement income plan that will help you achieve your financial goals and live the retirement lifestyle you've always dreamed of.

SOCIAL SECURITY

As you approach retirement, Social Security benefits become an important consideration in your overall financial plan. While Social Security benefits are not designed to provide all of your retirement income, they can still play a significant role in your financial well-being.

In this chapter, we will discuss how to maximize your Social Security benefits to ensure you receive the maximum amount of income possible in retirement.

Social Security benefits play an important role in retirement planning. For many Americans,

Social Security is a significant source of income in retirement, providing a foundation for financial stability.

However, understanding how Social Security benefits work and how to maximize them can be challenging. In this blog post, we'll provide an overview of Social Security benefits, discuss strategies for maximizing benefits, and provide tips for incorporating Social Security benefits into retirement planning.

Social Security benefits are calculated based on an individual's earnings over their lifetime. The Social Security Administration (SSA) calculates benefits based on a complex formula that takes into account an individual's highest 35 years of earnings.

The age at which an individual begins to receive benefits also affects the amount of benefits they receive. To be eligible for Social Security benefits, an individual must have earned at least 40 credits, or 10 years of work.

Early retirement can reduce Social Security benefits, while delaying retirement can increase benefits. For example, an individual who begins receiving benefits at age 62 will receive reduced benefits compared to an individual who delays receiving benefits until age 70. Other factors that can impact Social Security benefits include income from non-Social Security sources and disability.

There are several strategies for maximizing Social Security benefits. One strategy is to delay receiving benefits until age 70. For each year an individual delays receiving benefits past full retirement age (which is currently 66 or 67, depending on the year of birth), their benefits increase by 8%. Delaying retirement can be particularly beneficial for individuals who expect to live a long time.

Let's look at a client named Bob (made up name). He has over $700,000 saved in an investment account and retired at 65. His full social security wasn't until almost 67. Bob feared delaying social security and taking income from his account, as his Advisor told him there would be market risk weighing down his balance along with the 4% to 5% he withdraws.

Instead, Bob made the decision to work with me on the Retirement Parachute. He has delayed taking social security until beyond his full retirement age simply because he's now confident in his guaranteed 5% income stream of $35,000 annually from his Retirement Parachute account.

$700,000 x 5% lifetime income = $35,000 annually

Even if Bob's account goes down due to not keeping up with the withdrawals, he will still earn $35,000 annually!

If that's not a parachute, I don't know what is! We will discuss this more in chapter 7 when we define this Retirement Parachute some more.

Maximizing earnings is another strategy for maximizing Social Security benefits. This can be achieved by working for at least 35 years, as the SSA calculates benefits based on an individual's highest 35 years of earnings. Additionally, individuals can consider working past their full retirement age, as earnings after full retirement age can increase benefits.

Spousal and survivor benefits can also be a valuable source of income in retirement.

Spousal benefits allow a spouse to receive a portion of their partner's Social Security benefits, while survivor benefits provide income to a surviving spouse after the death of their partner.

It's important to note that some individuals may be subject to the Windfall Elimination Provision (WEP) or Government Pension Offset (GPO), which can reduce Social Security benefits for individuals who receive pensions from non-Social Security covered employment. It's important to understand how these provisions may impact Social Security benefits when planning for retirement.

Incorporating Social Security benefits into retirement planning is crucial. The SSA provides online tools, such as the Retirement Estimator and the Benefit Calculator, that can help individuals estimate their Social Security benefits. It's important to regularly review retirement plans and adjust strategies as needed, particularly as retirement approaches.

Social Security benefits are an important source of income in retirement. Understanding how Social Security benefits work and how to maximize them can help individuals achieve financial security in retirement.

By delaying retirement, maximizing earnings, and taking advantage of accounts without risk to guarantee income, can increase their Social Security benefits.

Incorporating Social Security benefits into retirement planning is crucial, and regularly reviewing retirement plans can help ensure financial stability in retirement.

2 Phases of Retirement

Retirement planning is an important aspect of long-term financial planning. It involves determining the amount of money needed to live comfortably in retirement and developing a plan to save and invest towards that goal.

The retirement process can be divided into two distinct phases:

The accumulation phase and the distribution phase.

The accumulation phase is the period leading up to retirement, during which individuals focus on saving and investing for their future. This phase typically lasts for several decades, during which time individuals aim to accumulate as much wealth as possible.

They may contribute to employer-sponsored retirement accounts such as 401(k) plans or individual retirement accounts (IRAs), as well as invest in stocks, mutual funds, or other high-risk assets.

During the accumulation phase, individuals may be more willing to take on higher levels of risk in order to potentially achieve higher returns. However, this can come with the risk of significant losses, particularly if the market experiences a downturn.

To mitigate this risk, it's important to diversify investments across different asset classes and consider investing in both domestic and international markets. This can help to reduce the overall level of risk in a portfolio, while still providing the potential for some growth.

As individuals approach retirement, they must begin to shift their focus from accumulation to income.

This is where the distribution phase comes into play.

The distribution phase is the period after an individual has retired and is no longer actively working. During this phase, the primary goal shifts from accumulation to income, as individuals begin to draw on their savings and investments to fund their retirement expenses. This phase can last for several decades, during which time individuals must be strategic about how they distribute their assets to ensure that their savings last throughout their retirement.

One of the biggest challenges during the distribution phase is managing the risk of outliving one's savings. This can be particularly difficult given the uncertainties of life expectancy and market performance.

To mitigate this risk, individuals may consider strategies such as the Retirement Parachute, which provide a guaranteed stream of income in retirement. This can provide a level of security and stability during retirement, ensuring that individuals have a steady income stream to cover their expenses.

Another important factor to consider during the distribution phase is tax planning. This is particularly important for individuals who have accumulated significant wealth in retirement accounts, such as 401(k) plans or IRAs.

Withdrawals from these accounts are generally subject to income tax, which can significantly reduce the amount of money available for retirement expenses. To minimize the impact of taxes on retirement income, individuals may consider strategies such as Roth conversions, which involve converting traditional retirement accounts into Roth accounts, or using other tax-advantaged investment vehicles.

In addition to tax planning, individuals must also be strategic about how they manage their retirement expenses during the distribution phase. This may involve creating a budget to ensure that expenses are kept in check, as well as being mindful of spending decisions.

One of the biggest risks during the distribution phase is overspending, which can significantly reduce the amount of money available for future expenses. To mitigate this risk, individuals may consider working with a financial advisor to develop a retirement income plan that takes into account their individual goals and needs.

Overall, the key to a successful transition from the accumulation phase to the distribution phase is to have a clear understanding of one's financial goals and to be proactive about adjusting investment strategies and spending habits as needed.

We will cover more in the next chapter about minimizing market risk which is an important factor in the distribution phase.

MITIGATING MARKET RISK IN YOUR RETIREMENT

As you approach retirement, your priorities shift from accumulating wealth to preserving it. One of the most significant risks you face in retirement is market risk. Market volatility can be devastating to your retirement savings, especially if you are relying on those funds for retirement income.

That's why it's important to understand how to invest for retirement in a way that mitigates market risk.

The main issue I see facing newly retired people is that they believe their investments and strategies have worked to get them this far, so "it's fine the way it is". The old saying of "what got you here won't get you there" certainly applies here.

You are now in preservation mode, not accumulation.

One way to mitigate market risk is to diversify your investments across different asset classes. You can diversify by investing in stocks, bonds, and cash. Stocks have historically provided the highest returns, but they also come with the highest risk.

Bonds are generally considered safer investments, but they also have lower returns. Cash investments, such as Money Market Savings, or savings accounts, provide the lowest returns, but they also have the lowest risk.

Keep in mind that diversifying among different asset classes REDUCES your risk, but does not ELIMINATE The risk. I also hear this very often with new retirees, claiming that their advisor has them in a "balanced portfolio". That's a great strategy, but keep in mind that there is still risk involved since it's invested in securities.

A balanced portfolio just means you may have less risk, but how much are you willing to take on? That's a rhetorical question, as only you can answer that.

Could you stomach losing 15%? Maybe 20%? If you have $500,000 saved up, then 20% is $100,000! That's a lot of money. Too often, Advisors and clients talk percentages, but you need to look at your dollar amount.

Let's take 2008 as an example. That was the year of the the credit crisis and housing market collapse. Imagine if someone was a few years away from retiring or just retired. The market lost about 38% that year! Let's say you saved up $500k for retirement to generate $25k of income each year to supplement your social security.

Now your $500k became $310,000 and can generate with the same 5% withdrawal rate, just $15,500!

This means you need to either work longer or find more money in order to generate more income. This is why if you take on market risk, you can't time the market, you never know when a bad downturn will occur.

Percentages isn't what puts bread on the table or keeps the lights on, dollar amounts are. The dollar amount from example above is a loss of $190,000.

It's also important to know that when you lose money, you need more to get back to where you were. Reason being, you have less capital in the account working for you.

As an example, in 2008, many people lost 35% or so in the market that year, and I heard many people say that they just need 35% and they will be back to where they were. Look at the chart below and you can see that you would need more than 35%

.

Digging A Hole
Small losses are easier to recover from, compared with big drops

Initial loss	Gain needed to recover
8%	8.7%
25	33
30	43
40	67
50	100

One investment option that can help mitigate market risk is the Retirement Parachute. It provides a fixed rate of return and the potential for additional interest based on the performance of an underlying index, such as the S&P 500. This can offer you a degree of market participation without the downside risk that comes with direct equity investments. You also can get guaranteed income streams, which can be an attractive option for retirees.

Avoiding market risk is crucial when it comes to retirement income. When you're in the accumulation phase of your financial journey, you can afford to take on more risk because you have time on your side. However, in retirement, you don't have the luxury of time, and market downturns can be especially damaging to your portfolio.

The Limitations of the 4% Rule for Retirement Income

When planning for retirement, it's important to have a strategy for generating income that will sustain you throughout your retirement years. One commonly used rule of thumb for determining a safe withdrawal rate is the 4% rule.

The 4% rule suggests that you can withdraw 4% of your retirement portfolio in the first year of retirement, and then adjust that amount for inflation each year thereafter. While this rule may sound simple and straightforward, it's not without its limitations.

The 4% rule was developed based on historical stock and bond returns, and assumes that you will have a balanced portfolio of stocks and bonds. The idea is that by withdrawing 4% of your initial portfolio value each year, you will be able to generate enough income to last throughout a 30-year retirement, while also accounting for inflation. However, there are several reasons why the 4% rule may not be a good fit for everyone.

First, the 4% rule assumes that your portfolio will generate an average return of 7% or more over time. This assumption may not hold true in today's low-interest-rate environment, which could make it difficult to achieve the same level of returns that were seen in the past.

In addition, the 4% rule does not account for the sequence of returns risk, which refers to the potential for a negative return in the early years of retirement. If you experience a market downturn early on in your retirement years, and still need to withdraw, it could significantly reduce the value of your portfolio and leave you with less income to support your needs over time.

Take a look at the image below. These are the same annual returns for two different people, but in reverse order. Jane has early negative returns and therefore her portfolio after 15 years of 4% withdrawals ends up with just $74,300 remaining.

Meanwhile you can see Jim's portfolio on the right with positive returns early and the negative returns at the end, winds up with $344,290 left after the same 15 years of 4% withdrawals annually!

This simply tells us that the 4% rule can be very unreliable because we don't know when and which returns will hit.

JANE'S PORTFOLIO
WITH EARLY NEGATIVE RETURNS
Beginning Balance $500,000

Age	Return	Annual Withdrawal	Growth	Ending Value
66	-10.14%	$20,000	$(48,672)	$431,328
67	-12.04%	$20,500	$(53,572)	$357,256
68	-23.37%	$21,012	$(78,580)	$257,664
69	26.38%	$21,537	$62,290	$298,417
70	8.99%	$22,075	$24,843	$301,185
71	3.00%	$22,627	$8,357	$286,915
72	13.62%	$23,193	$35,919	$299,641
73	3.53%	$23,773	$9,738	$285,606
74	-38.49%	$24,367	$(100,551)	$160,688
75	23.45%	$24,976	$31,825	$167,537
76	12.78%	$25,600	$18,140	$160,076
77	0.00%	$26,240	—	$133,836
78	13.41%	$26,896	$14,341	$121,281
79	29.60%	$27,568	$27,739	$121,452
80	11.39%	$28,257	$10,615	$103,810
81	0.73%	$28,963	$(546)	$74,300

Ending Balance $74,300

JIM'S PORTFOLIO
WITH LATE NEGATIVE RETURNS
Beginning Balance $500,000

Age	Return	Annual Withdrawal	Growth	Ending Value
66	-0.73%	$20,000	$(3,504)	$476,496
67	11.39%	$20,500	$51,938	$507,934
68	29.60%	$21,012	$144,129	$631,051
69	13.41%	$21,537	$81,736	$691,250
70	0.00%	$22,075	—	$669,175
71	12.78%	$22,627	$82,629	$729,176
72	23.45%	$23,193	$165,553	$871,537
73	-38.49%	$23,773	$(326,304)	$521,459
74	3.53%	$24,367	$17,547	$514,640
75	13.62%	$24,976	$66,692	$556,356
76	3.00%	$25,600	$15,923	$546,679
77	8.99%	$26,240	$46,787	$567,226
78	26.38%	$26,896	$142,539	$682,869
79	-23.37%	$27,568	$(153,144)	$502,157
80	-13.04%	$28,257	$(61,797)	$412,104
81	-10.14%	$28,963	$(38,850)	$344,290

Ending Balance $344,290

Another limitation of the 4% rule is that it assumes a static spending rate. In reality, your spending needs may change over time. You may have unexpected expenses, such as healthcare or home repairs, that could require a larger withdrawal from your portfolio.

Conversely, you may be able to reduce your spending in later years of retirement, which would allow you to withdraw less from your portfolio. The 4% rule doesn't provide the flexibility to adjust your spending in response to changing circumstances.

Finally, the 4% rule assumes that you will have a relatively stable retirement income. However, many retirees today may have more unpredictable sources of income, such as part-time work or rental income, which can make it difficult to determine a safe withdrawal rate from their portfolio.

Life expectancy is another topic that Advisors today don't discuss with the 4% rule. It doesn't account for changes in life expectancy. People are living longer than ever before, and it's becoming increasingly common for individuals to live well into their late 80s and 90s.

If someone retires at age 65 and follows the 4% rule, they may be withdrawing money from their retirement savings for 30 years or more. That's a long time to sustain a steady income without the possibility of running out of money.

Overall, while the 4% rule may be a useful starting point for retirement income planning, it's important to recognize that it has limitations. To ensure a sustainable retirement income, you may need to consider other strategies, such as a more dynamic spending plan or the use of financial products, like annuities, that can help to reduce sequence of returns risk and provide a more reliable stream of income.

An alternative to the 4% rule is to use a retirement income product such as the Retirement Parachute. It can provide a guaranteed stream of income for the rest of the retiree's life, regardless of market conditions. While this strategy may come with fees or other limitations, they can offer peace of mind and help retirees avoid the risk of outliving their retirement savings.

In conclusion, while the 4% rule has been a popular guideline for retirement income planning, it's not a one-size-fits-all solution. It's important to consider individual circumstances, market conditions, and the potential for inflation and increased life expectancy when planning for retirement income. By doing so, retirees can increase their chances of maintaining a steady income throughout their retirement years.

THE BENEFITS OF ROLLING OVER OLD 401(K)S TO IRAS

As you near retirement, it's important to take a closer look at your retirement accounts, including your 401(k)s. You may have several old 401(k) accounts from previous employers that you've forgotten about. Consolidating these accounts by rolling them over to an IRA has many benefits, including increased control over your investments, lower fees, and simplified recordkeeping.

Retirement savings is an essential part of financial planning. One of the most common retirement savings options available to employees is a 401(k) plan. However, once an employee leaves their job or retires, they must decide what to do with their 401(k) savings.

One option is to roll it over to an Individual Retirement Account (IRA). Let's explore the benefits of rolling over a 401(k) to an IRA.

What is a 401(k) rollover?

A 401(k) rollover is a process in which an individual moves their retirement savings from a 401(k) plan to an Individua Retirement Account (IRA). The IRA can be an existing account or a new one opened specifically for the rollover. The process involves withdrawing the funds from the 401(k) plan and depositing them into the IRA. The individual must complete the rollover within 60 days of withdrawing the funds to avoid taxes and penalties.

A direct transfer can also be done, which is easier to conduct since it goes from custodian to custodian and you don't need to handle any checks or worry about the 60 day rule.

Increased Investment Control

One of the biggest advantages of rolling over an old 401(k) to an IRA is increased investment control. With a 401(k), you're typically limited to the investment options provided by your employer. When you roll your funds over to an IRA, you have access to a much wider range of investment options, including stocks, bonds, mutual funds, exchange-traded funds (ETFs), or even the Retirement Parachute.

This gives you greater control over your investment strategy and allows you to choose investments that align with your retirement goals, risk tolerance, and investment preferences.

If you have multiple old 401(k) accounts, keeping track of them can be a hassle. When you roll them over to an IRA, you'll have just one account to manage, which can simplify recordkeeping and make it easier to keep track of your investments.

Lower Fees

Another advantage of rolling over old 401(k)s to an IRA is lower fees. 401(k)s often have higher fees than IRAs, which can eat away at your retirement savings over time. With an IRA, you have more control over the fees you pay, and you can shop around for low-cost options.

Working with a Financial Advisor is even more cost effective than most 401k's, since they are very high in fees.

More Flexibility with Distributions

When you reach age 72, you're required to start taking required minimum distributions (RMDs) from your retirement accounts. If you have multiple 401(k) accounts, you'll need to take an RMD from each one.

However, if you roll your 401(k)s over to an IRA, you can take the RMD from just one account, which can simplify the process and help you avoid potential penalties for missed distributions.

Regular withdrawals before 72 are also easier out of your own account. Many employers may have lengthy withdrawal forms or process in order to make a simple withdrawal. I don't know about you, but I don't want to ask my former employer for "permission to take out money".

Ability to Convert to a Roth IRA

If you're interested in converting some or all of your retirement savings to a Roth IRA, rolling over your old 401(k) to an IRA can make the process easier. You can roll your funds over to a traditional IRA and then convert the account to a Roth IRA, which can provide tax-free income in retirement. However, it's important to note that converting to a Roth IRA can result in a large tax bill, so you'll want to work with a financial advisor to determine if this strategy makes sense for your unique situation.

What Is The Retirement Parachute?

As you move closer to retirement, you may start to feel a sense of uncertainty about the future.

How much money will you need to live comfortably in retirement?

What happens if you outlive your savings?

What if the market crashes and your investments lose value?

These are all valid concerns, and it's important to have a plan in place to help you achieve a secure retirement.

One concept that can help you navigate the complexities of retirement planning is the Retirement Parachute. This term refers to a financial strategy designed to help ensure a safe and comfortable landing in retirement. Just as a parachute helps a skydiver land safely, a retirement parachute can help protect your retirement savings and provide a reliable source of income throughout your retirement years.

The key components of the Retirement Parachute include guaranteed income, principal protection, and growth potential.

Guaranteed income can come from sources such as Social Security, pensions, and annuities. These sources provide a predictable stream of income that you can rely on throughout your retirement years.

Principal protection, as the name suggests, means protecting your retirement savings from losses due to market downturns or other factors.

Growth potential means that your retirement savings should have the potential to grow over time, helping to keep pace with inflation and ensure that you have enough money to last throughout retirement.

One financial product that can help provide all of these components is the indexed annuity. This type of annuity offers a guaranteed minimum interest rate, along with the potential to earn additional interest based on the performance of a market index such as the S&P 500.

Indexed annuities also offer downside protection, which means that your principal is protected from losses due to market downturns.

With an indexed annuity, you can have the potential for growth without the risk of losing your principal.

Just like you wouldn't build a house on a foundation that isn't secure, why build your retirement on something that isn't secure?

If you are getting social security income, you already have one part of the Retirement Parachute. A pension can serve as another, and lastly, an Indexed Annuity.

They all have a couple things in common:

- The income is typically for the rest of your life

- The stock market doesn't affect your income

It's important to note that indexed annuities are not suitable for everyone. They may be more appropriate for those who are in or near retirement and looking for a conservative investment option that can provide a reliable source of income.

An indexed annuity is a liquid investment, but not as liquid as a savings account or stocks, meaning that it is designed to be held for a specific period of time, typically 5-10 years or longer. If you need access to your money before the end of the surrender period, you may be subject to surrender charges and other fees.

This is why I never instruct anyone to put 100% of their liquid money into indexed annuities, but rather take a balanced approach with the "income producing" portion of their money going into this bucket.

In addition to indexed annuities, there are other financial products and strategies that can help you build something close to a retirement parachute. For example, diversifying your investments across different asset classes can help reduce risk and increase your chances of success. Working with a financial professional can also help you create a comprehensive retirement plan that addresses your unique needs and goals.

Now let's look at Indexed Annuities closer

Market Risk & Potential Return

Indexed annuities are designed to protect investors from market risk in several ways:

1. **Guaranteed Minimum Interest Rate:** Indexed annuities typically offer a guaranteed minimum interest rate that is paid regardless of how the un-

derlying stock market index performs. This means that even if the index performs poorly, the investor is guaranteed to earn at least the minimum rate of return.

2. **Participation Rate:** Indexed annuities also have a participation rate, which is the percentage of the index's performance that the annuity will credit to the investor's account. For example, if the participation rate is 80% and the index gains 10%, the investor would earn an 8% return. However, if the index loses value, the investor's account value will not decrease.

3. **Caps and Floors:** Indexed annuities may also have caps and floors, which

limit the amount of returns an investor can earn in a given period while also protecting them from losses. Caps limit the maximum return that an investor can earn, while floors protect against losses by ensuring that the investor's account value will not drop below a certain level, even if the index loses value.

Basically, you are earning a portion of the upside in exchange for now downside risk.

Guaranteed Income Rider

Indexed annuities can offer guaranteed income payments to investors through a feature called a guaranteed income rider. A guaranteed income rider is an optional add-on feature to an indexed annuity that provides a guaranteed income stream during retirement.

The investor pays sometimes pays an additional fee to add the rider to their indexed annuity. There are some companies that offer the income rider for free.

In exchange, the rider guarantees a certain level of income payments to the investor for a specified period, typically for the rest of their life.

The guaranteed income payments are calculated based on the value of the investor's annuity account and the payout rate specified in the rider.

The payout rate is typically a percentage of the account value, ranging from 3% to 7%, depending on the investor's age and the terms of the annuity contract.

The guaranteed income rider provides a predictable income stream to the investor, regardless of how the stock market performs.

Now let's look at a real example:

Jane retired with $300,000 and wanted a predictable income stream for the rest of her life. She gets an Indexed Annuity that will pay her 5% of her initial amount, or higher, for the rest of her life. Jane only wanted to supplement her income by about $1,000 a month.

So, $300,000 x 5% = $15,000, which is $1,250 per month.

If at the end of 5 years, her balance is $340,000, then 5% of $340,000 is now $17,000 annually, or $1,416 per month!

Jane just got a raise by her balance being higher.

Let's say Jane's account after 5 years is now instead worth $225,000. In any other investment, she would be getting only about $11,000 annually, or $937 monthly!

But with an Indexed Annuity income rider, she is still getting 5% based on her initial amount of $300,000.

What if her balance winds up at zero one day?

That's a great question, and the answer is, she'll still keep getting $15,000 each year!

Now that's what you called a parachute!

So, basically, rather than having your money go up and down with the market, what if you can have something like this below?

$100,000 hypothetical investment in two options

Year	A. Investment *including risk*		B. Variable rate *with no risk*	
1	9%	$109,000	5.5%	$105,500
2	12%	$122,080	8%	$113,940
3	-30%	$85,456	0%	$113,940
4	17%	$99,983	13%	$128,752

You can see that investment A with risk winds up under its starting investment! The second account, which is an indexed annuity, for the same 4 years, winds up at $128,752.

This isn't because indexed annuities get higher returns, it's because they avoid market loss!

So, the Retirement Parachute to guarantee you the needed income for retirement and give you a secure, worry free retirement is:

- Social Security Income

- Pension

- Indexed Annuity with Income Rider

If you are younger, you can still accumulate a great retirement income by contributing regularly to an indexed annuity or rolling over an old 401k and letting it grow until retirement age without risk due to the market.

Retirement Healthcare: Preparing for and Managing Healthcare Costs in Retirement

One of the most significant expenses that retirees face is healthcare costs. According to recent studies, a couple who retires at 65 years old can expect to pay over $250,000 in healthcare expenses over the course of their retirement. With this in mind, it's critical to prepare for and manage these costs as you plan for retirement.

In this chapter, we will explore some of the ways that you can prepare for and manage your healthcare costs in retirement.

Understand Your Medicare Options

Medicare is the primary healthcare coverage for individuals aged 65 and over. However, it does not cover all healthcare costs, and the costs that it does cover can vary depending on the plan you choose.

It's important to understand your Medicare coverage and the costs associated with it, including premiums, deductibles, and co-payments. You may also want to consider purchasing supplemental insurance to help cover costs that Medicare doesn't.

There are four parts to Medicare: A, B, C, and D. Medicare Part A covers hospital stays, while Medicare Part B covers doctor visits, outpatient care, and preventive services. Medicare Part C is also known as Medicare Advantage, which is a combination of Parts A and B. Part D covers prescription drug coverage.

It's crucial to research and understand which Medicare plans are best for your individual needs and budget.

Here are some tips for preparing for and managing healthcare costs in retirement.

Plan for Long-Term Care

Long-term care refers to the services and support that individuals may need as they age or due to disability or incontinence. It is estimated that 70% of people over 65 will require long-term care at some point in their lives. Long-term care can be expensive, and Medicare does not cover most long-term care services. In fact, Medicare only covers the first 100 days of skilled care, but after those 100 days, you're on your own.

According to US News, as of 2022, the average cost for a nursing home is over $108,000 a year! This will put a dent in anyone's retirement savings.

It's important to have a plan in place to cover these costs, such as purchasing long-term care insurance or considering other options, like a life insurance policy with long-term care benefits.

Utilize Health Savings Accounts (HSAs)

Health savings accounts (HSAs) are accounts that individuals can use to save money for healthcare expenses. These accounts are only available to individuals who have a high-deductible health plan (HDHP).

Contributions to HSAs are tax-deductible, and withdrawals for qualified medical expenses are tax-free. HSAs can be an effective way to save money for healthcare expenses in retirement and can also serve as an additional retirement savings account.

Many go into retirement already having high balances in their HSA. While you do have options with those accounts, you can also utilize those funds for your healthcare costs.

Manage Chronic Health Conditions

Chronic health conditions can be costly to manage, and they can significantly impact your retirement savings. It's essential to take care of your health and manage any chronic conditions to reduce your healthcare expenses.

Some ways to manage chronic conditions include eating a healthy diet, exercising regularly, and following your doctor's orders for medications and treatments.

As we age, healthcare becomes an increasingly important aspect of retirement planning. According to recent studies, healthcare costs in retirement are rising faster than the rate of inflation, and Medicare may not cover all of the expenses that retirees may face.

Plan for Prescription Drug Costs

Prescription drugs can be a significant expense in retirement. Medicare Part D covers prescription drugs, but there are out-of-pocket costs associated with it, such as deductibles and co-payments. It's important to review your medication needs and consider that your healthcare costs will be higher than anticipated because of prescription costs.

Part D drug plans offer good coverage but have coverage gaps, called donut holes. This means that each year, you only have a certain amount of coverage.

How to Protect and Transfer Your Wealth with Estate Planning

Retirement planning is a critical aspect of financial planning that many people prioritize as they approach retirement age. However, one essential component of retirement planning that often goes overlooked is estate planning.

Estate planning is the process of creating a plan to transfer your wealth and assets to your loved ones after you pass away. It is a vital step to ensure that your assets are distributed according to your wishes and that your loved ones are taken care of after you are gone.

Creating a will is one of the first steps in estate planning. A will is a legal document that outlines how you want your assets to be distributed after you pass away. It also allows you to name an executor, the person responsible for managing the distribution of your assets according to your wishes.

Without a will, your assets will be distributed according to your state's laws, which may not reflect your wishes.

This is why creating a will is crucial to ensure that your assets go to the right people and are distributed as you intended.

Another crucial document to consider as part of your estate plan is a trust.

There are several different types of trusts that can be used in estate planning. Each type of trust has its own unique features and benefits, and choosing the right type of trust depends on your specific goals and circumstances.

1. **Revocable Living Trust** - A revocable living trust is a trust that you create during your lifetime and can be changed or revoked at any time. It allows you to maintain control of your assets during your lifetime and provides for the distribution of those assets after your death. This type of trust can help you avoid probate and keep your affairs private, while still allowing you to make changes to your plan if your circumstances change.

2. **Irrevocable Living Trust** - An irrevocable living trust is a trust that cannot be changed or revoked once it is created. This type of trust can provide sig-

nificant tax benefits and asset protection, but it also requires you to give up control of your assets. An irrevocable trust can be used to remove assets from your estate and reduce your estate tax liability, or to protect assets from creditors or legal claims.

3. **Testamentary Trust** - A testamentary trust is a trust that is created in your will and takes effect after your death. This type of trust can be used to provide for minor children, protect assets from spendthrift beneficiaries, or provide for a surviving spouse. A testamentary trust does not provide the same benefits as a living trust, but it can be a useful tool in certain circumstances.

4. **Special Needs Trust** - A special needs trust is a trust that is designed to provide for the needs of a disabled or incapacitated beneficiary without affecting their eligibility for government benefits. This type of trust can be used to provide for medical care, housing, and other necessities without jeopardizing the beneficiary's eligibility for programs such as Medicaid or Supplemental Security Income.

5. **Charitable Trust** - A charitable trust is a trust that is created to benefit a charitable organization or cause. This type of trust can provide significant tax benefits for the donor, while also supporting a cause that is important to them. There are several different types of charitable trusts, including chari-

table remainder trusts and charitable lead trusts, each with its own unique features and benefits.

While each type of trust has its own unique features and benefits, they all share some common characteristics. Trusts are legal entities that can own and manage assets, and they can be used to provide for the needs of beneficiaries both during and after the lifetime of the creator of the trust.

One of the main benefits of creating a trust is that it can help you avoid probate. Probate is the legal process that takes place after someone passes away to distribute their assets. It can be a long and expensive process, and it's often public, which means anyone can access information about your assets and how they are distributed.

By creating a trust, you can transfer your assets to your beneficiaries without going through probate, which can save time and money, and help keep your affairs private.

In addition to creating a will and trust, there are other critical steps to take as part of your estate planning. For example, it's important to name beneficiaries for your retirement accounts and life insurance policies. These assets pass directly to the named beneficiaries and do not go through probate.

It's also important to keep your estate plan up to date, especially after major life events like marriage, divorce, or the birth of a child.

One significant reason to avoid probate is the typical fees associated with it. Probate can be a lengthy and costly process, with legal fees and court costs that can quickly eat away at the value of an estate.

The probate process can also be time-consuming and emotionally draining for the loved ones left behind. Creating a will can provide clarity and guidance for loved ones during a difficult time. A will can help to avoid confusion and conflict over how assets should be distributed, and it can give the deceased person a sense of control over their legacy.

It's essential to work with a qualified estate planning attorney to create a will and/or trust that meets your specific needs and goals. An attorney can help you understand the various estate planning tools available and can guide you through the legal requirements and formalities involved in creating and maintaining these documents.

They can also help you navigate complex estate planning issues such as minimizing estate taxes, ensuring asset protection, and naming guardians for minor children.

Summary

Congratulations! You've made it to the end of this guide on securing your retirement with the Retirement Parachute. Hopefully, the information and strategies presented in this book have helped you feel more confident and prepared for your retirement years.

Now that you have a better understanding of the Retirement Parachute, it's time to take action. One of the best things you can do is to meet with a financial advisor who specializes in retirement income.

A qualified advisor can help you evaluate your current financial situation, identify your goals, and create a customized retirement plan that fits your unique needs. I'm biased, but I'd love to offer you a demo and illustration of this at work for you.

If you're interested in learning more about the Retirement Parachute, you can also do a complimentary review with me. This review will help you determine whether or not the Retirement Parachute is the right option for you and your retirement goals.

You can email me at flavio@cfgcarolina.com with questions. You can also book an appointment by going to BookWithCFG.com

Remember, the Retirement Parachute is all about providing you with a secure and worry-free retirement. With careful planning, smart investments, and a focus on protecting your assets, you can rest easy knowing that you're prepared for the future.

Afterword

I hope you've enjoyed the information in this book to help secure your retirement. As you can see, there are many ways to secure your income.

If you'd like a review of your situation at no obligation, send me an email at flavio@cfgcarolina.com

If you'd like more information about the agency in Myrtle Beach, visit CFGCarolina.com or CoastWealthGroup.com

And lastly, feel free to email me at flavio@cfgcarolina.com with any questions, press inquiries, or speaking inquires.

www.ingramcontent.com/pod-product-compliance
Lightning Source LLC
Chambersburg PA
CBHW070301220526
45465CB00004B/1704